ONE THOUSAND
PAPER CRANES

W9-BZW-033

ONE THOUSAND PAPER CRANES

The Story of Sadako and the Children's Peace Statue

Published by
Dell Laurel-Leaf
an imprint of
Random House Children's Books
a division of Random House, Inc.
1540 Broadway
New York, New York 10036

If you purchased this book without a cover you should be aware that this book is stolen property. It was reported as "unsold and destroyed" to the publisher and neither the author nor the publisher has received any payment for this "stripped book."

Photographs contributed by Takayuki Ishii, Ichiro Kawamoto, Masahiro Sasaki, Kiyo Ohkura, Marie Bogart, and the Hiroshima Peace Memorial Museum

Illustrations by Sarah Carlson

Copyright © 1997 by Takayuki Ishi

All rights reserved. No part of this book may be reproduced or transmitted in any form or by any means, electronic or mechanical, including photocopying, recording, or by any information storage and retrieval system, without the written permission of the Publisher, except where permitted by law. For information address Yohan Publications, Inc., 14-9, Okubo 3-chrome, Shinjuku-ku, Tokyo, Japan.

The trademark Laurel-Leaf Library® is registered in the U.S. Patent and Trademark Office.
The Trademark Dell® is registered in the U.S. Patent and Trademark Office.

Visit us on the Web! www.randomhouse.com/teens
Educators and librarians, for a variety of teaching tools, visit us at www.randomhouse.com/teachers

ISBN: 0-440-22843-3
RL: 6.0
Reprinted by arrangement with Yohan Publications, Inc.
Printed in the United States of America
January 2001
OPM 20 19 18 17 16 15 14 13 12

Contents

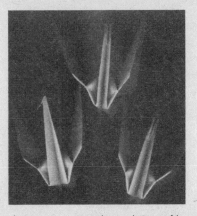

In Japan the crane is a traditional sign of long life and good fortune. According to the folk tale, if one crane represented a thousand years of happiness, then a thousand cranes would mean one million years of happiness.

ONE THOUSAND
PAPER CRANES

Introduction

One day in the fall of 1991 my son Scott, then a fifth grader, came home from school, quite excited, and asked me if I had ever heard about the story of Sadako. At first, I didn't recall it because in Japan, Sadako was known as "the girl who folded paper cranes," and not by her first name. As my son explained the story to me, I recognized it. Coincidentally, my family and I were planning to visit Japan the following spring. Scott pleaded with me to take him to Hiroshima so he could see Sadako's statue. This was the beginning of a journey which would end with my writing this book.

When we returned from our visit to Hiroshima in April 1992, I read several books about Sadako, in addition to numerous other books on Hiroshima and Nagasaki. When I had finished reading all the available material I could find on Sadako, I decided to write a fact-based book on Sadako for the children of America and other English-speaking children of the world.

My decision to write this particular book was primarily because of my interest in children. Children represent our future, and I believe that children and youth are a vital part of our present society. Young and old, we all must work together for a better society.

In discussing the horrors of the atomic bombs that were dropped on Hiroshima and Nagasaki, people frequently say, "Let's not forget Pearl Harbor!" They are right—we must remember Pearl Harbor, but we must also remember Hiroshima, Nagasaki, the Holocaust, all the horrors of World War II, the Korean War, the My Lai Massacre in Vietnam, and all the other atrocities of wars throughout history. The real issue as I see it is not who or which country committed what crime, but why! Every war invariably results in terrible tragedies, immense waste and sinful destruction. All wars, no matter how big or small, how nearby or far away, diminish our humanity to a barbaric level.

Why Sadako's story? Because the story of Sadako goes beyond the issue of world peace and beyond the horror of the atomic bomb. It is a story well worth telling and, hopefully, well worth reading. Even a brief familiarity with this courageous young girl will reveal a person of exceptional character. Those who knew her soon discovered that she was a uniquely gifted child, able to confront adversity gracefully and be strong against the many hardships she had to endure. It can be safely assumed that a person of less courage, subjected to a similar ordeal, would not have survived as long and bravely as she did.

But we must keep in mind another important aspect of this poignant story. From the very beginning, Sadako's painful and prolonged burden was lightened appreciably by the unwavering support she received from her devoted family, friends, and teacher. In their supportive roles, they all played heroic parts. And finally, who among us would not be uplifted to learn about a small group of young students who miraculously and almost single-handedly turned a beautiful dream into an awe-inspiring reality?

In my effort to write a fact-based book, I realized that it would be highly advantageous if I could see for myself where and how the story began. This could only be successfully achieved if I had first-hand knowledge of the facts, most of which could only be obtained in Japan . . . the home of Sadako Sasaki!

In 1993 and in 1996, I revisited Hiroshima and Nagasaki. From the first day of my visit I felt overwhelmed by the hospitality and cooperation that was extended to me by every member of the Sasaki family, which includes Sadako's father and mother, her older brother Masahiro, his wife Yaeko, and their daughter Tomoyo. I met Eiji, Sadako's younger brother, at the cemetery. I never did get to meet Sadako's younger sister Mitue, because she lived a distance away from her family, in Fukuoka.

During my first visit with the Sasakis, I frequently walked, talked, and dined with them. They showed me many photographs of Sadako and gave me a number of paper cranes which Sadako had actually folded during her stay in the hospital.

Sometime later, we went to visit the family grave where Sadako's remains are buried. Even before my visit came to an end, I felt as though these lovely people were now a part of my extended family.

I also met Kiyo Ohkura, who had been Sadako's roommate at the hospital. She gave me very valuable personal information about Sadako, which was previously not known to the public. Ms. Ohkura is now a high school librarian in Tokyo.

I also had the good fortune to meet with Mr. Ichiro Kawamoto, who played a major role in helping to build the Children's Peace Statue, *Genbaku-no-Ko-no-Zoh* (the Statue for the Children of the Atomic Bomb). He is now retired from his job as custodian in the Hiroshima Jogakuin Junior and Senior High School for Girls. To this very day, along with a small group from the Hiroshima Paper Cranes Association, he takes care of the Children's Peace Statue and makes certain that it always looks its best. Mr. Kawamoto also cares for the monument that honors the many Koreans who were victims of the atomic bomb. At the time of the bombing, a great number of Koreans were in Hiroshima as forced laborers. Many of them died.

This book would truly be incomplete if I did not mention my gratitude to the following for their generous and helpful support.

My wife Jeannette: I shall always remember her constant support and encouragement. My son Scott, whose idea gave me the jump start I needed. Mr. Alen Gascone, Mr. Mark Dunn, Ms. Lee Ebs, Ms. Helen Borrello and Ms. Sarah Strawn for their editorial help and Ms. Sarah Carlson for her illustration work. And finally Ms. Marie Bogart who typed and prepared the manuscript for the publisher.

Plus . . . all the new friends, associates, advisors and supporters I made in Japan and in the United States.

Thank you all.
TAKAYUKI ISHII
April 1997

Sadako, the first grader

Preface

"Let's build a peace statue in America, like Sadako's statue in Japan!" This is the cry that echoed throughout the classrooms in the Arroyo del Oso Elementary School of Albuquerque, New Mexico, in February 1990.

That possibility became a reality when the model for the American Children's Peace Statue, "Our Hope For A Peaceful Future," was built and dedicated in August 1995 in Albuquerque on the fiftieth anniversary of the creation and dropping of the atomic bomb. The model was chosen in May of 1994 at Bradbury Science Museum in Los Alamos, New Mexico. Just as the children and youth involved in the Japanese movement had been instrumental in seeing Sadako's statue become a reality, so the children in this country with the help of adult advisors played their own pivotal role in the American movement.

On the occasion of the erection and dedication of the Children's Peace Statue in Albuquerque, I hoped all of us—young and old—would come to understand and resolve never to forget the hor-

Sadako's parents, 1993

rendous effects of the nuclear bomb demonstrated too vividly in Hiroshima, Nagasaki, the Bikini Islands, the Marshall Islands, and all other parts of the world suffering from nuclear tests.

Building this Children's Peace Statue in close proximity to such a symbolic site as Los Alamos, where the first atomic bomb was created, will forever remind people everywhere that our dream is world peace. Peace must prevail.

The story of Sadako and the Children's Peace Statue will help us to understand in depth exactly what happened on August 6, 1945, in Hiroshima; what happened on that day to the Sasaki family; how Sadako survived; how Sadako came to fold her paper cranes; and how the Children's Peace Statue came to be built in Hiroshima Peace Memorial Park.

On a clear spring day, May 5, 1958, in a small park in Hiroshima, thousands of children solemnly unveiled their memorial honoring Sadako Sasaki (born January 7, 1943; died October 25, 1955). The memorial also commemorates the thousands of other children who died from the explosion of the atomic bomb and its horrendous aftereffects. This simple stone memorial dedicated to and erected by the children of Japan has become a symbol of peace throughout the world.

Ten years after the atomic bomb was dropped on Hiroshima, twelve-year-old Sadako died in the hospital bed to which she had been confined for the last eight months of her life. In serene silence, without a tear, without a murmur, her eight months of pain and suffering came to a merciful end.

Sadako's courageous struggle for life and her undying faith evidenced by folding one thousand paper cranes inspired her classmates and people throughout Japan, both young and old, to erect a statue to remember her and the many other children who died as a result of the bomb. This Children's Peace Statue is now known throughout the world as the Statue for the Children of the Atomic Bomb (*Genbaku-no-Ko-no-Zoh* in Japanese).

Every year, thousands of visitors make pilgrimages to the memorial to honor the memory of the children who died as a result of the atomic bomb and its aftermath. In silence, people place colorful paper cranes at the foot of the memorial statue.

I hope that the reader will be inspired to join the ever-widening circle of those who choose to follow Sadako's example by folding paper cranes, and by working for world peace.

one

ATOMIC BOMB
and RADIATION

Between 1941 and 1945, Japan was involved in the Second World War, a conflagration that engulfed most of the world. In 1945, the end of the war was drawing near, and Japan, Germany and Italy were facing defeat by the Allied Forces, including the United States and Great Britain. All of Japan's major cities were under constant aerial bombardment. Large squadrons of heavy B-29 bombers repeatedly firebombed Tokyo, Yokohama, Osaka and Nagoya.

Most of these cities became seas of fire as a result of these bombings. Upon impact, a typical firebomb spread an intensely hot, burning oil-like substance over large areas, destroying everything it touched. At the time, most Japanese houses were constructed entirely of wood, so they were easily ignited and quickly burned to the ground. Many houses were intentionally destroyed to make empty spaces to slow down the spread of fire throughout Japan.

Meanwhile, scientists in the United States were creating a far more devastating bomb—the world's first atomic bomb. The first atomic bomb was developed in Los Alamos, New Mexico, and passed its first test on July 16, 1945. The U.S. Army had already targeted a Japanese city for the first bombing.

Hiroshima was the first choice, Kokura the second choice, and Nagasaki, the third. These cities were chosen because they were manufacturing centers of military equipment in the Japanese war effort. U.S. military leaders determined that a clear, cloudless day would be most suitable for this mission.

The atomic bomb which was dropped in Hiroshima produced a very large amount of radiation. Sadako's death, ten years after the Hiroshima bombing, was caused by radiation exposure.

Radiation can't be seen, but it's like light; it penetrates and permeates everything and everyone that is near it. Once exposed to radiation, even a small degree of it, living things will begin to deteriorate and will eventually die. In some cases, radiation sickness progresses in the human body slowly over a long period of time. Such was the case for Sadako.

Due to the severity of the radiation over Hiroshima and Nagasaki, it was believed by many scientists that no trees, grass, vegetation or human life would be able to live in these cities for a hundred years.

two

AN UNFORGETTABLE MORNING

On August 6, 1945, the weather over Hiroshima was hot, clear and bright. At early dawn suddenly air raid alarms alerted the population, and thousands went into hiding. The cause of this particular alarm proved to be a U.S. Air Force weather reconnaissance plane checking out conditions over Hiroshima. At 7:32 A.M., the all clear alarm sounded, and people once again resumed their normal routines. They did not know that the pilot of the reconnaissance plane had radioed back to his bomber command headquarters that the weather was perfect for their mission.

That same day, as clear skies broke over the U.S. bomber base on Tinian Island near Guam, a lone U.S. B-29 bomber named the *Enola Gay*, carrying a bomb named Little Boy, was warming up for take-off. The world had crossed a threshold into an atomic age of potential total destruction. At about the same time, the lifting of the air raid alert in Hiroshima made people feel a sense of relief, convincing them that there would be no air strike on that day. With her engines ready, the *Enola Gay* took off and headed directly for Hiroshima. In her bomb-bay compartment she carried a single bomb.

Unaware of the destiny which awaited them, the residents of Hiroshima went about their day-to-day affairs. As in numerous other cities, many of these residents were systematically tearing down a number of houses to limit the spread of fire in the heavily populated areas. Approximately ten thousand individuals were at work in these areas that morning, including eight thousand boys and girls from junior and senior high schools.

Flying approximately twenty-eight thousand feet above her target, the *Enola Gay* silently released her deadly cargo. Seconds later, at 8:15 A.M., the entire city of Hiroshima was blanketed by a burst of brilliant light. A violent wind, intense heat and a deafening sonic boom rapidly followed, as if the city had been dropped into the bowels of hell. This was but one moment of that fateful day. For the first time in history, humankind was to be threatened by the unpredictable wrath of the atomic bomb.

The center of the bomb was above the building now most popularly known as the Atomic Bomb Dome. The bomb actually exploded in the air less than one half mile above the city, and immediately produced 7,232 degrees of heat at ground level.

To understand how intense this heat was, we only have to remember that water boils at about 212 degrees Fahrenheit, and that iron will begin to melt at 2,732 degrees.

Due to the enormous heat, everything within a half-mile radius of the hypercenter was either seriously damaged or destroyed. All glass items and tile roofs melted. Almost every wooden structure within a mile-and-a-half radius of the bomb instantly burned to the ground. Every man, woman and child for miles around was either killed or seriously injured or burned.

Almost every person not inside some structure at the time of the bombing died instantly. Those who survived suffered extensive burns over large

Atomic Bomb Dome
(Hiroshima Peace Culture Foundation)

areas of their bodies. Because it was August, people were wearing lightweight clothing, short pants and short sleeves. This added greatly to the severity of the burns.

The immense force of the explosive wind ravaged the city with greater casualties and damage. In the immediate area of the hypercenter, the velocity of the wind was recorded at 1,444 feet per second. One half mile from the hypercenter, it was recorded at 525 feet per second, and at two miles away, 98 feet per second.

With wind speed far exceeding that of gale force, nearly every home and structure within a radius of two miles was totally demolished. Clouds of flying debris and burning shrapnel added to the horrible scene of destruction. Just hours after the smoke, heat, wind and fires had subsided, the destructive aftermath of the explosion began to claim its toll. Like a contagious disease, the horror of radiation spread cancer throughout the city.

The widespread, lingering aftereffects of the radiation made the effects of the bomb more deadly. Immediately after the explosion, while the bombed area was still saturated with radiation, thousands of people from the surrounding areas of the city rushed in to find their loved ones in the burning and contaminated rubble. Emergency rescue crews and medical teams frantically came to the aid of the stricken. Tragically, many of them eventually fell victim to the radiation also. The people

1/2 mile
3/4 mile
1-1/2 miles

Hiroshima City after the bombing
(Hiroshima Peace Culture Foundation)

who worked and lived in Hiroshima were totally unprepared for the devastation that would level four and a half square miles of their city. No conventional bomb known to humanity at the time could have achieved the destructive force that was unleashed by the atomic bomb.

Men, women and children who at first showed no visible symptoms from the bombing soon became extremely ill with persistent bleeding from the mouth and ears. Purple marks appeared on var-

17

ious parts of their bodies, caused by massive internal bleeding. Huge areas of flesh would blister and fall off. Infections were common and virtually unresponsive to conventional treatment. The once proud and prosperous Hiroshima had become a city of nightmares.

At the time of the bombing, it was estimated that Hiroshima's population was approximately 370,000. Casualty figures resulting directly from the explosion itself—that is, instantaneous deaths—are subject to contention. But it was reported by the Hiroshima Prefecture in August 1946 that the death total was 118,661. This number did not include soldiers, and therefore the true death count was probably closer to 150,000. There is no final figure, of course, because even now the number of dead continues to increase with each passing year.

As noted before, the world's first atomic bomb was dropped over Hiroshima. It was called Little Boy. The second bomb was dropped over Nagasaki three days later. Interestingly, it was called Fat Man.

three

A DESPERATE ESCAPE

Aioi Bridge
(Hiroshima Peace Culture Foundation)

In 1945, the Sasaki family included two-year-old Sadako, her 26-year-old mother Fujiko, her four-year-old brother Masahiro, her 66-year-old grandmother Matsu, and her father, 28-year-old Shigeo, who was away from home, serving in the military.

The family lived in Kusunoki-cho, a residential area about a mile north from the hypercenter.

Minutes before 8:15 A.M. on August 6, 1945, the Sasaki family was at home eating breakfast as usual.

Suddenly a neighbor called out loudly, "Mrs. Sasaki . . . Come out of the house . . . Look up there . . . Beautiful things are floating down from the sky." Mrs. Sasaki immediately rushed outside. Looking up, she saw three small, glittering parachutes slowly descending to the ground. Thinking them of no special importance, she returned to her family and continued with breakfast. Moments later, the sky exploded with a blazing flash of blinding white light.

Immediately after the blinding flash came the booming sound of the explosion, which was rapidly followed by violent gushes of wind from all directions. Within minutes of the explosion most of the homes in Kusunoki-cho, including the Sasakis', were completely demolished. The entire area as far as one could see had become an unrecognizable wasteland.

As Mrs. Sasaki was digging out from the debris of her house, she heard Sadako outside calling for her. Mrs. Sasaki rushed outside toward the voice and frantically searched through the rubble. She found Sadako in the backyard sitting, fearfully, atop a wooden box that had originally been on the second floor of the house. Mrs. Sasaki embraced her tearful daughter. As she was comforting Sadako, her thoughts turned to the rest of the family. Sadako was uninjured, but what about her son Masahiro and her mother-in-law Matsu . . . where were they? Were they lying somewhere nearby injured or possibly dead? With her mind racing with fear and confusion, she picked up Sadako and carefully carried the frightened child past the debris into what was left of her severely damaged home. After calling out several times, she found her son, covered with debris, under the kitchen table. The force of the explosion had apparently flung Masahiro into a bunch of *tatami* mats and lodged him safely under the kitchen table. Grandma Matsu was also located nearby. She had a slight injury to her left hand, but aside from this minor injury, the Sasakis were alive and intact, albeit very much in a state of shock.

Mrs. Sasaki had heard of the terrible fire raids over Tokyo, Yokohama, Osaka and Nagoya, and she assumed that Hiroshima was now experiencing its first fire bombing. Determined to remove her fam-

Hiroshima City
(Hiroshima Peace Culture Foundation)

ily from further danger, she alerted them to get ready for immediate evacuation. She snatched up little Sadako and, carrying the child on her back, took a small cloth bag of essentials that was already prepared for emergencies such as this. She proceeded to lead her frightened, disheveled family out of their crumbling house.

Now, acutely aware of how dangerous the situation was, she was determined to gather her family and take them to a safe place and as far away as possible. As she looked up and saw the spreading mushroom-shaped cloud ominously hovering in the sky, she began to doubt that there was such a thing as a safe place any more.

Struggling to keep her mind focused on the safety of her family, Mrs. Sasaki led them to the nearby Ohta River, hoping to get to Ohshiba Park. She hoped to find refuge in the rescue and evacuation center there that had been set up to handle serious air raids and emergencies. They inched their way through smoldering debris, mangled corpses, and confused, injured masses. Mrs. Sasaki tried to keep her children from seeing the enormity of the human suffering and destruction which surrounded them.

They soon found themselves part of a growing column of wailing people, walking, stumbling and crawling towards the river. Many of them had lost their hair from fire. Many more were burned beyond belief. Others were bleeding from wounds inflicted by flying glass. Those few who were not seriously injured were trying their best to rescue the hundreds who were trapped under the fallen debris.

Everywhere Mrs. Sasaki went, she heard the desperate cries for help and constant screams of pain. Men, women and children continued their exhausting trek toward Ohshiba Park.

At some point Grandma Matsu suddenly remembered that she had left a sizable packet of cash in a hidden place at home, and told Mrs. Sasaki that she must return home to get it. Mrs. Sasaki tried to change her mind, but to no avail. Saying that she would meet them later at the park, Grandma Matsu said goodbye and started on her return journey. Mrs. Sasaki, Sadako and Masahiro continued on their way.

Normally, it would take about five minutes to reach the Misasa Bridge, the bridge closest to Sadako's house. This day, the trip took about a half hour, a long, painful, unforgettable half hour. Because of the intensity of the heat and fire, some people started to panic and rushed headlong into the river, trampling those who stood in their way.

From horizon to horizon, the sky had started to turn black and the air seemed to boil with heat, making it difficult to breathe. Black, tar-like dust covered the landscape like a shroud. As the fire spread closer and closer to the river, the heat became unbearable. Fearing the possibility that they might be burned to death, Mrs. Sasaki drew her children closer to her, doing her best to comfort them. Silently she prayed for salvation from this plague from hell.

When the Sasakis reached the river bank, a man in a small boat stood up and started yelling, "Mrs. Sasaki, Mrs. Sasaki . . . over here . . . Quick, get into the boat." Mrs. Sasaki recognized the man as an old family friend. At first, she was reluctant to board the boat, because it was already overloaded with people, and it seemed that it might sink. But with each passing moment the fire and heat became more unbearable, so she decided to take the chance and went aboard with her family.

With Mrs. Sasaki and her children on board, the small craft moved slowly toward the middle of the river, trying to avoid the intense heat which was coming from the shore. As the overloaded boat bobbed among the floating dead, Mrs. Sasaki worried that it would sink or catch fire.

Adding to her fear was the dense, coal-like soot which continued to rain down on them. "What is it? Where does it come from? Will this hurt us?" she wondered. As conditions worsened, Mrs. Sasaki's fear approached a state of panic. She couldn't help thinking that the end of her life was near and even that the end of the world had come. She tried her best to shield her children from the ugly black rain that continued to shower down on them.

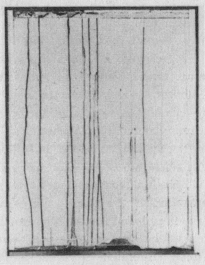

Black Rain
(Hiroshima Peace Memorial Museum)

Finally, the black dust diminished and the sky slowly began to clear and recapture some of its light. The black rain that fell over Hiroshima and saturated the area for miles around was the dreadful contaminated dust of nuclear radiation.

After about two hours, conditions improved to a point where people on the boat felt safe to return to shore. Bloated corpses floated aimlessly on the river like dead fish. As they came ashore, they saw dead bodies by the hundreds lying grotesquely one on top of the other. Mrs. Sasaki covered her young children's eyes.

The noxious odor of charred bodies was everywhere. In a matter of minutes all of the Sasakis' senses were brutally assaulted with the stench of death. With each step, she could feel the heat from the scorched earth coming through the soles of her shoes. With Sadako bound to her back and Masahiro firmly in hand, Mrs. Sasaki continued on her way, more determined than ever to reach Ohshiba Park.

When they finally reached the park, their hopes of finding refuge vanished. They had gone from one hell to another. What was once a beautiful oasis was now a wasteland of helpless refugees stumbling about in confusion and despair. Mrs. Sasaki's motherly instinct to save her children helped her block out the many desperate cries for help and the endless wails of pain which threatened to shatter her remaining links to sanity.

Standing in the middle of all of this human devastation and confusion, she employed what little strength she had left to search for Grandma Matsu. Sick at heart and weak with hunger and fatigue, Mrs. Sasaki reluctantly ended her search for Matsu. She found a small, leafless tree still standing in the corner of the park. She placed her children under its scorched branches and sat down.

Several hours later, as evening approached, Mrs. Sasaki heard some comforting voices in the distance. They were the voices of rescue teams coming from areas that had been relatively untouched by the bomb. As soon as the teams reached the suf-

ferers, they began to distribute food and medical aid. Unfortunately, both of these items were in short supply. Each person received only one *onigiri* (riceball). Mrs. Sasaki hadn't thought about food all day, but when she saw the *onigiri* she realized how hungry she was.

Shortly after their arrival, the rescue teams formed a small caravan of trucks to take a limited number of people to Miyoshi, a small city about forty miles from Hiroshima. Mrs. Sasaki's parents lived close to Miyoshi and now, thinking only of the safety of her children, she was most anxious to see them. She knew that regular transportation by train or bus would not be available, but she was in no condition to walk forty difficult miles with two small children. Gratefully, she accepted the ride to Miyoshi and quickly boarded one of the over-crowded trucks with her two children.

The ride was extremely slow and uncomfortable, but they arrived safely later that evening in Miyoshi. After a short walk, the tired, disheveled and hungry Sasakis reached the doorstep of Mrs. Sasaki's parents. Mrs. Sasaki's father and mother were over-joyed to see their daughter and grandchildren safe and unharmed. The warm welcome Mrs. Sasaki received, combined with the assurance that the family was finally in a safe place, brought tears of relief to her eyes.

After a few days of relative calm, the uprooted Sasakis were reunited with Mr. Sasaki, who had been in the Hiroshima area as a member of the rescue team. When he discovered that his family had gone to his in-laws' house, he immediately joined them. A short time later the family returned to what was left of their home and slowly began the task of rebuilding. Though they had survived the actual bombing, all of them would, in time and in varying degrees, suffer from the bomb's hideous aftereffects.

The Sasakis learned about a week later that Grandma Matsu was dead. She had died on her way back to the home. Her body, covered with burns and the marks of radiation poisoning, was found near the house by a rescue team.

The Sasakis and their neighbors went back to the land they owned and built simple temporary houses. Life was difficult, but they had each other. In November, Mrs. Sasaki became very ill. With each passing day, the radiation that had infected her body would make its gruesome symptoms more visible. Soon, it became apparent that Mr. Sasaki was also infected. Both parents took consolation in thinking that at least Sadako and Masahiro had been spared what was now commonly referred to as the Atomic Bomb Disease. Sadako in particular was a very healthy, active young girl.

four

SADAKO'S ILLNESS

Now, nine years later, with the war behind them, the Sasaki family, like so many other Japanese families, had begun to rebuild and plan for the future. Mr. Sasaki opened a small barber shop in Hatchobori in downtown Hiroshima. As the years passed, the Sasakis increased the size of the family by two: Mitsue, a girl, and Eiji, a boy.

Masahiro, the older son, was now a seventh-grader at Nobori-cho Junior High School, and Sadako was a sixth-grader at Nobori-cho Elementary School. For the Sasakis, life was once again very near the way they wanted it—peaceful and happy. Healthy, vibrant, athletic and very popular at school, Sadako enjoyed sports, especially running. She won almost every race she competed in, and soon became the star runner in the Bamboo Class of her school. In Japan, each elementary school class is given a unique name; Sadako's was the Bamboo Class. She even outran most of the boys.

In May, there was a mini field day. The Bamboo Class finished in last place in the relay race. They dropped the baton several times. As a result, Mr. Nomura, the teacher of the Bamboo Class, spent months coaching the runners to improve the exchange of the baton. He said to the team, "We cannot depend only on Sadako. We must improve the baton exchange." After months of practice, and because they had Sadako on their team, the team was quite confident that they would win in the coming Grand Field Day.

Sadako
Bamboo Class Relay Team

Sadako herself relates her experiences on the Grand Field Day in an essay she wrote shortly after the event:

ANXIOUSLY AWAITING THE GRAND FIELD DAY.

October 15, 1954.

I waited for this day . . . a very special day, because I would be running in the relay races. Our teacher told us that we should not eat or drink before the race. I also went to the bathroom many times to lighten my body weight. Now it was time for the long-awaited relay race, the main event of the day. I was very nervous even before our team prepared to go to the starting line. The first runners were all in the starting position. At the crack of the pistol they all took off. As my turn approached, I saw Miss Najime in second place but as she approached me she passed the number one runner and was now in first place. I knew that my mother was watching, so as I took the baton from Miss Najime, I ran as fast as I could to please her. I finished my turn and was so relieved, and heard the final crack of the pistol which meant the end of the relay race. We won! The Bamboo Class had won with a commanding lead. Everyone was cheering our victory. I was so very, very happy. Everywhere I looked I saw smiling faces.   *Sadako Sasaki.*

During the winter recess in December, not long after the Grand Field Day, Sadako started to com-

Grand Field Day
Sadako and her parents

plain of a general discomfort. There was also a painful swelling under her ears. Thinking that it might be the initial symptom of the mumps, Sadako's mother took her temperature. There was no fever.

When Sadako's condition persisted, her father became worried and decided to take her to see Dr. Hatagawa. In addition to being the family pediatrician, Dr. Hatagawa was also one of Mr. Sasaki's regular customers at the barber shop.

When Dr. Hatagawa completed his examination, he consulted with Sadako's parents in private.

Gravely, he said, "Sadako was exposed to *Pika*, wasn't she?" (People in Japan referred to the atomic bomb as *Pika Don. Pika* means a paralyzing flash; *Don* means roaring blast.) "I am recommending that she go to the A.B.C.C. for a complete check-up."

The A.B.C.C. (Atomic Bomb Casualty Commission) was a special research center established by the United States government to monitor the effects of the atomic bomb explosions over Hiroshima and Nagasaki. All those who were exposed to the bombing were given a compulsory check-up by the A.B.C.C. every two years on their birthday. The entire Sasaki family—father, mother, Sadako and Masahiro always kept their appointments. Because Sadako's most recent check-ups showed negative, Mrs. Sasaki was reasonably certain that Sadako's recent symptoms were not related to the Atomic Bomb Disease.

Mrs. Sasaki told Dr. Hatagawa that Sadako had just had an examination at the A.B.C.C. in June and that the test results were negative. The doctor was still suspicious, however, and insisted that Sadako go for another check-up. Now both parents became very concerned about the doctor's insistent recommendation. They immediately made two appointments with the A.B.C.C., one for January 18, the second for February 16. Sadako had a complete exam, including blood tests and X rays.

Those tests showed that Sadako's white blood count was 33,000. A normal person's white blood count is between 5,000 and 8,000. Her red blood count was 3,560,000. A normal person's would be between 4,000,000 and 5,000,000. In the 1940s and 1950s very little was known about radiation and the multiple ways it affects the body. In addition to disfiguring surface burns (keloids), radiation from the atomic bomb also attacks vital organs, bones, and the circulatory and nervous systems. It produces a form of widespread incurable cancer, and it takes the form of fatal leukemia. In actuality, no part of the human body is immune from the tragic horror that results from radiation.

The human body contains two types of blood cells: red and white. The red blood cells circulate oxygen and nourishment throughout the body. White blood cells fight germs that invade the body. In a normal person, there is a vital balance between red and white blood cells. But when the body is infected with leukemia, the red blood cells are progressively destroyed, and eventually the body's immune system is left defenseless because the proper balance between red and white cells no longer exists. In the case of Sadako, her white blood cells were four times higher than normal, and her red blood cell count was rapidly decreasing.

On February 18, after Sadako had already left for school, the Sasakis received a phone call from Dr. Hatagawa asking Mr. Sasaki to come to his office immediately. By the tone of his voice, Mr. Sasaki suspected that it was not good news.

At the doctor's office, Dr. Hatagawa told Mr. Saski that the report from the A.B.C.C. revealed some irregular activity in Sadako's blood cells, and it seemed to be due to *Pika*. The doctor went on to explain to Mr. Sasaki that he was quite certain that Sadako had leukemia, which was undoubtedly caused by radiation. Mr. Sasaki was stunned. He couldn't believe what he had just heard. "Sadako has leukemia . . . radiation," he kept repeating in sorrowful tones in the doctor's office. He immediately recalled a newspaper article about a boy the same age as Sadako who had died of leukemia, as a result of exposure to atomic bomb radiation. "How serious is Sadako's condition?" he asked. "Please tell me the truth."

Grimly, the doctor replied, "I am very sorry, Mr. Sasaki. She may have only three months, possibly a year."

Mr. Sasaki turned pale. He tried desperately not to show his grief. Repeatedly, as in a death-like trance, he kept saying to himself, "Sadako is going to die. My little girl is going to die. How could this happen? How?"

Dr. Hatagawa said that it was very important to get Sadako to the hospital immediately. His words did not reach Mr. Sasaki, who sat overcome with grief. Later that day, when he finally arrived home, Mr. Sasaki couldn't even remember how he had gotten there. As he walked through the front door, Mrs. Sasaki, who had been anxiously awaiting his return, realized that the news wasn't good: her husband's sad expression gave it away. She asked, "What did the doctor say?"

Slowly, Mr. Sasaki raised his head and in a halting voice delivered the tragic news: "Sadako has leukemia. She has only three months to live, possibly a year! It's *Pika* . . . It's all because of *Pika*! I am going to her school to bring her home. Dr. Hatagawa says we must get her to the hospital as soon as possible."

As he turned to leave, Mrs. Sasaki said, "Wait a minute, Shigeo. I have something I must do." Quickly she gathered up the money they had been saving and gave it to him. With tear-filled eyes, she said, "Please buy a pretty kimono for Sadako. It will be her first and she's always wanted one." Wearing one's own kimono is every girl's dream in Japan, and Sadako was no exception.

What little extra money the family had managed to save did not come easy. The modest barber shop had cost them all the money they had and more. Buying the material for a kimono would be a sacrifice for them at this time, but it was one they would gladly make. It would be a surprise for their dying daughter Sadako! Mr. Sasaki put the money in his pocket and hurried out of the house with tears in his eyes.

When Mr. Sasaki arrived at Sadako's school he found his daughter standing alone, watching her classmates taking gym class. Mr. Nomura, her teacher, saw Mr. Sasaki come in and approached him. "Does Sadako need another check-up?" he asked. "We got the results back. She's got leukemia," Mr. Sasaki grimly answered. Mr. Nomura was shocked by the reply, especially since he was quite familiar with the seriousness of the disease. Mr. Sasaki went on to explain that Sadako had at most only one year left to live.

"Is she really that sick?" asked Mr. Nomura, as if he could not or would not believe what he had just heard.

Sadako was watching them from a distance and found herself thinking, "Oh no. It looks like I'm going to have to take another test at the A.B.C.C.." She remembered only too well how painful those

Sadako, showing her swelling.

spinal fluid injections were. Normally, Sadako was quite a brave girl who tolerated pain without complaining, but this time she wanted very much to avoid another test.

When Mr. Nomura finished talking to Mr. Sasaki, he went and placed his hand gently on Sadako's shoulder, turned to her classmates and said, "Sadako needs to be hospitalized." The entire class found it difficult to believe this sad announcement. Most of them remembered how healthy and robust Sadako had been only a few weeks before. Though Sadako was seriously ill, she didn't look very sick until the very end of her life.

Sadako was very sad at the prospect of being hospitalized. She loved her school and friends. One of her joys in waking up in the morning was to go to school. She always liked to be with people. She didn't even like saying goodbye to her classmates. She just waved her hand. Not being able to go to school saddened Sadako.

As they were leaving the school, Mr. Sasaki tried to conceal his real emotions and at the same time offer as much comfort as possible. "Don't worry, Sadako. It's not that serious. Once you're in the hospital you'll soon get better. Guess what? Today we are going to buy a kimono for you!"

"A kimono for me!" said Sadako in complete surprise. Confused, surprised, elated—her mind was churning with wonder. It's February 18. Nothing special about this day. It's not even close to New

Year's Day, the traditional time to give gifts. Sadako was well aware that her parents had little money and that kimonos were very expensive. "Daddy, I don't need a kimono, and besides, it's going to cost you a lot of money when I'm in the hospital."

"Don't worry about it . . . we had some extra money put aside, and Mom and I always wanted to get you one. Today is as good a time as any."

Once in the kimono shop, Mr. Sasaki looked around for material that would best suit his daughter. He and Sadako finally selected a very pretty fabric with a cherry blossom design. Though she had said earlier that she didn't want a kimono, once she saw how beautiful the material was, Sadako couldn't conceal her happiness. Mr. Sasaki beamed with pride at his daughter and said, "That one is perfect for you." With a big smile, Sadako nodded in total agreement.

As they started home, Mr. Sasaki turned to Sadako and said, "You only have swelling of the lymphatic gland. It's nothing to worry about. It will get better soon and before you know it, you'll be back in school." Sadako found her father's words very comforting, particularly the prospect of going back to school, and she did not hide her happiness from her father.

The next day the Sasakis received a phone call from the Red Cross Hospital. Sadako would have to go to the hospital on February 21, only two days away. Mr. Sasaki suggested that they all pack up and

go to his sister's house in Mihara. He knew that
once Sadako was in the hospital it would be difficult
to visit his sister. Sadako was thrilled at the thought
of seeing her aunt and very much looked forward
to the trip.

Mrs. Sasaki reminded everyone that Sadako's
aunt was especially good at sewing kimonos, so she

would ask her as a special favor to help sew a kimono for Sadako. The entire family decided to leave that very night for the two-hour train trip to Mihara. Having been informed of Sadako's condition, Sadako's aunt was anxiously awaiting their arrival. The Sasakis arrived that evening and were warmly greeted by everyone. After the children had eaten and gone to bed, Sadako's aunt and her daughter, along with Mrs. Sasaki, started on their labor of love: sewing a kimono for dear Sadako. As Mrs. Sasaki worked, she could not hold back the tears.

The next morning Sadako awoke and went into the main room to greet her parents and her aunt. She immediately saw it, a beautiful kimono with cherry blossom designs. Sadako stood, totally speechless, admiring the finished garment with childlike wonder. "Put it on, Sadako," her mother said.

At first Sadako was a little shy as she hesitatingly slipped into the soft kimono. She was afraid that everyone was watching her, which they were. Now Sadako stood in front of the mirror, admiring herself and the new young lady-like image she was seeing for the first time. A kimono was indeed a miraculous thing . . . especially if it had cherry blossoms and adorned a pretty young girl like Sadako!

five

SAYONARA, MY DEAR FRIENDS

On February 20, 1955, the day before she entered the Red Cross Hospital, Sadako along with her sister Mitsue and Mr. Sasaki went to the school to say goodbye to her classmates. Her classmates were practicing relay races, but when Sadako arrived, they all gathered, and said their goodbyes to Sadako. They promised Sadako that they would visit her at the hospital.

The next day, February 21, Sadako entered the hospital. At the time she was admitted, there were no beds immediately available, so she was temporarily placed in the emergency room. Her condition had already progressed to such an advanced state that the doctors felt it essential to administer treatment immediately. Additional tests confirmed what was originally diagnosed: malignant acute marrow leukemia. This type of leukemia deteriorates the body rapidly and is incurable.

In early March, Sadako was transferred to a regular ward. As was expected, her condition worsened.

Sadako's treatment was extensive. She had to undergo constant blood transfusions, in addition to repeated injections of cortisone to keep her white cell count down. But these efforts were only meant to treat the symptoms of leukemia, not to cure it. The treatments were also very costly; a single blood transfusion cost 180 dollars and one injection of cortisone cost 300 dollars. In the month of March alone, Sadako's hospital bill ran over 4,000 dollars. In the same period of time the average worker's salary in Japan was about 1,900 dollars a month.

Sadako, despite her youth, was keenly aware of her parents' financial situation. She wondered how they were going to pay the enormous hospital bills. Mrs. Sasaki told her daughter not to worry about such matters, that the important thing was to get better. Sadako heeded her mother's advice. "I'll do whatever the doctors say, Mommy," Sadako told her mother, "and I'll do my best to get better. I want to go back to school!"

On March 16, the sixth-grade Bamboo Class held a graduation party at the school. Happily, Dr. Numata, a hospital physician at the Red Cross Hospital, gave Sadako permission to attend. The thought of going to a party and seeing all her classmates made Sadako extremely happy. For the first time in weeks, Sadako's parents saw a smile on her face.

Now Sadako had the perfect opportunity to wear her newly-made kimono. As she arrived at the party, her classmates couldn't help staring in admiration at Sadako in her beautiful kimono. The girls gathered around her and pleaded, "Can we touch your kimono? You look so pretty, Sadako!" The boys showed their approval by clapping their hands. Sadako had become a celebrity and was enjoying every minute of it.

As soon as the party started Sadako was given the center seat, which was traditionally reserved for the guest of honor. As the students sang and watched skits, Mrs. Sasaki sat in the back of the room, sharing a rare moment of happiness with her daughter.

Sadako had to leave early because she became very tired. She graciously thanked everyone present. She tried her best not to cry in front of her classmates. As the boys and girls gathered around to say farewell, she couldn't help admiring her healthy friends. In a parting chorus, they all wished her well and promised to visit her in the hospital, saying "Sadako, get well soon!"

Mr. Nomura walked Sadako and her mother to the door and even outside. He held up a camera and said, "Sadako, you look so pretty in your kimono. Let me take a picture of you." After he took the picture, he stood at the gate and waved a long sorrowful goodbye. As Sadako turned to take one final look at her school, she saw many of her classmates standing at the school windows. They too

Sadako, in
her kimono

were sadly waving their goodbyes. Sadako started
to cry. With her tears, she could hardly see Mr.
Nomura, her classmates or the school building.

That bittersweet day of the graduation party was
the last time Sadako would see her beloved school.
Her condition was so unstable that Dr. Numata
could not permit her to attend the graduation ceremony. As a graduation gift, Sadako's classmates
gave her a pretty red notebook signed by all of
them and a *kokeshi* (wooden doll), which Sadako
kept at her bedside until her death.

In April 1955, Sadako was promoted to the
junior high school level. Although she was not permitted to attend the special ceremony for entering

junior high school, this did not prevent her from becoming an official seventh-grader at Nobori-cho Junior High School.

As time passed, Sadako began to show signs of slight improvement. It seemed that the concentrated treatment of transfusions combined with the cortisone injections were effective in decreasing her white blood cell count. The news of her slight improvement was just enough to lift the spirits of the Sasakis and give them a sense of hope.

In May, Sadako was moved to a semi-private room which she shared with Kiyo Ohkura, a recovering tuberculosis patient who was two years older than Sadako. Kiyo was not thrilled at first about hav-

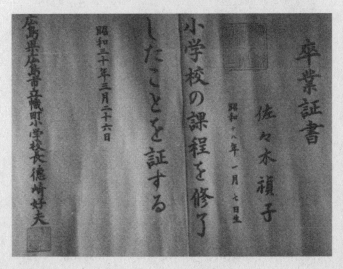

Sadako's graduation certificate

ing a younger roommate, but soon Kiyo and Sadako became close friends. The many happy moments the two girls shared helped Sadako to tolerate her unpleasant daily routine. Sadako followed Kiyo, calling her *O-ne-e-chan*, which is an affectionate and respectful term for older sister.

Sadako and her roommate Kiyo

Kiyo loved to read. Sadako, on the other hand, loved to socialize with other patients, old and young, and with the many nursing staff members throughout the hospital. As a result, a very shy Kiyo became acquainted with Sadako's friends in the hospital. "Sadako, you know everybody in the hospital. I'll call you a 'mayor' of this hospital," said Kiyo.

Sadako, Kiyo and friends
at the Red Cross Hospital

One day Sadako asked Kiyo if she could borrow some of Kiyo's books. One of the books which Sadako enjoyed reading involved romance. Almost a teenager, Sadako began to show interest in romantic relationships between a man and a woman. The little book was difficult for Sadako to understand, but she enjoyed reading it, and asked Kiyo many questions about love.

Unfortunately, the Sasakis faced serious financial difficulty. They not only had to pay enormous hospital bills, but they also had to pay their neighbor's debt. Mr. Sasaki was a very kind person who often helped his friends' businesses. He had co-signed a neighbor's loan, and the neighbor's business went into bankruptcy. Now Mr. Sasaki was

51

responsible for repaying the loan. Eventually the Sasakis were forced to sell their house.

On the day before they had to move, Sadako was given special permission to sleep at home for one evening. The house was not luxurious, but for Sadako it held many pleasant memories, and she relished this one last chance to recapture some of them. That night she cried herself to sleep. The next morning, the family moved to a smaller house in the Moto-machi district of Hiroshima.

six

MY FRIEND YUKIKO

Unfortunately, Sadako's improvement was short-lived. In June, a sudden reversal took place, and her condition became worse than before. In addition, her friend Yukiko, who was also being treated for leukemia, died. Yukiko was only six years old, born after the atomic bomb was dropped. However, both her parents had been exposed to it. Sadako thought of her as a little sister.

Sadako and Kiyo went to the room where Yukiko was laid to say their goodbyes. They were shocked to see her face discolored with so many purple marks, which often occur in advanced stages of leukemia. After seeing the terrible symptoms of leukemia on Yukiko's face, Sadako stopped suddenly on the way back to their room and said to Kiyo, "Am I going to die like that?" "Don't worry, Sadako. It's not going to happen to you," said Kiyo. Then she held Sadako firmly in a comforting hug.

As they embraced, Kiyo noticed how bony Sadako's body felt. Just as they were about to get into their beds, they looked out the window. It was raining heavily.

By the next evening, the rain stopped. As they looked out the window, they decided to go to the rooftop. They said to each other, "The brightest star we find will be Yukiko's!" In Japan, children are often told that when people die, they go to heaven and become one of the stars in the sky.

Since Sadako was an intelligent and sensitive girl, it was only natural that she eventually came to suspect that she was infected with the Atomic Bomb Disease. One day when Mr. Nomura and her friends from school came to visit her, she told them about the terrible effects of the Atomic Bomb Disease. She began to dwell on her sickness and retreat within herself. It became increasingly apparent to those around her that she had an intuitive sense about her fatal condition. As her symptoms intensified and her health deteriorated, Sadako began to ask frightening questions of herself, "Will I die soon? How much longer will I live?" A grim, relentless reality had pulled back the curtain for Sadako to see her tragic fate. For a twelve-year-old girl who found so much joy in living, it was an especially painful experience.

In July, Sadako's white blood count shot up to a dangerous level. Her gums now bled often as her condition worsened. However, it would still be difficult to guess how very sick she was just from her appearance. She walked around the hospital and socialized with many patients, often playing with little children, so that some adult patients asked, "What illness does she have? She is so pleasant and kind to little children."

One day Sadako happened to hear some adult patients with the same condition as hers talking about their symptoms. One of them said, "If you have a white blood cell count over 100,000, that would be fatal." She became very frightened when she heard this, but at the same time, was determined to find out what her white blood cell count was.

Sadako had become quite friendly with most of the nursing staff who worked on her floor. She frequently visited their stations to chat with them. She also knew where the patients' charts were kept. One evening all the nurses on her floor were called away on a serious emergency. Seeing the nurses' station completely unattended, Sadako took advantage of the situation by sneaking into the station and copying down the figures from her chart. She knew what she was doing was wrong, and felt a strong sense of guilt, but when she discovered that her blood count was not as serious as she had thought, 30,000 at its peak, she was relieved.

Sadako attended the August 6th Peace Ceremony with her family. They attended every year and participated in the ceremony of a thousand floating lanterns, each holding a lighted candle symbolizing that the spirit of the dead will live forever, to remember the victims of the atomic bomb. The next day, Sadako came back to the hospital quite excited, and said to Kiyo, "*O-ne-e-chan*, I learned a new song at the Peace Ceremony yesterday. Do you want to hear it?" Sadako, who had a very beautiful voice, started to sing "*Genbaku O Yurusumaji*" (We will never again allow the atomic bomb). Kiyo said to Sadako, "It's beautiful, Sadako! I could hear that music from the roof-top of the hospital yesterday. I wanted to learn that song myself. Thanks for teaching me the song." Sadako was so proud that Kiyo was really enjoying learning the song.

Sadako was a very talented young girl. She could not run anymore as she used to, but she sang all the time. Sadako also loved to take care of the younger children in the hospital. They often looked all over the hospital for Sadako. No wonder Kiyo called her the "mayor" of the hospital.

seven

FOLDING PAPER CRANES

A few days after the Peace Ceremony, a nurse came into Sadako's room, carrying a chain of folded paper cranes. "Look, Sadako, aren't these pretty? A girl from a high school in Nagoya sent hundreds of them to our patients. I thought you and Kiyo might like to have these paper cranes." Sadako and Kiyo were very happy to get them. Sadako remembered a story which her mother had told her several years ago: if you fold a thousand paper cranes, your wish will come true. So Sadako said to Kiyo, "*One-e-chan*, let's fold paper cranes!" "Okay," said Kiyo, and together they started on their new project of folding paper cranes.

At first they used any kind of paper they could find, but eventually they settled on the square sheets of paper used by the hospital to wrap powdered medicines.

"I will fold one thousand cranes, starting right here and now," said a determined Sadako.

Now Sadako had a mission. She would fold a thousand paper cranes all by herself and her wish would be granted. Sitting straight up in bed she vigorously folded the cranes. She was determined not to let anything stop her from reaching her goal. It soon became evident that a single source of paper would not be enough for her to achieve her goal, so she doggedly searched for every piece of paper she could find, including scraps of candy wrappers and gift wrap. Sadako had placed her chains of folded cranes all over her room, hanging down from the ceiling.

"Sadako, you fold cranes very nicely and so very fast!" said Kiyo.

Sadako replied, "I must fold them. I've got to finish a thousand of them if I'm going to get better."

There were days when Sadako wasn't feeling well, but she continued faithfully to fold the cranes.

During one of his visits in mid-August, Mr. Sasaki noticed how pale and drawn his daughter looked. "Sadako, you look tired. Why don't you put aside the cranes and rest?"

"It's okay, Papa. I have a reason for folding them. If I finish folding a thousand of them, I believe that my wish to be healthy again will come true."

Unfortunately, as time passed and the number of cranes grew larger, Sadako's condition did not improve, and her pain and discomfort increased. In spite of this, Sadako continued folding the cranes with her resolute belief that she would get better.

Sadako's worsening condition prompted Mr. Sasaki to ask Dr. Numata to allow his daughter to spend weekends at home with her family. Knowing Sadako had only a limited time to live, Dr. Numata consented to Mr. Sasaki's request.

Mr. Sasaki was both anxious and elated on the third Saturday in August when he went to pick up Sadako at the hospital. For Sadako, this weekend stay at home was almost as good as being discharged from the hospital. Her spirits soared as she took her father's hand and walked as fast as she could toward home. "Did folding paper cranes make this all possible?" she wondered.

As Sadako and her father reached the house, the entire family could hear the bells that were attached to her favorite handbag. They welcomed Sadako with great joy: "Sadako! *Oka-e-ri-na-sai!*" (Welcome home.) Now Sadako and her family had something very special to look forward to every weekend. On one weekend, Sadako came home with gifts for everybody, which were purchased at the hospital gift shop. Sadako's relatives had given her gifts of money, which she saved to buy presents for her parents, two brothers and sister. Sadako was a very considerate and kind-hearted young girl. The family made the most of these two-day visits, because they knew the time would soon come when there would be no more.

Sadako's purse, where she
kept her paper cranes.

Sadako and her brother, Eiji.

Even though these weekend visits home were like a good medicine for Sadako, her condition continued to decline. By the end of August her body was covered with large purple marks and her gums were constantly bleeding. Despite her declining condition, she had completed folding one thousand cranes. She was very happy with her accomplishment, but she was too weak to even consider a celebration.

In early September, Sadako's roommate and dear friend Kiyo was pronounced cured and was discharged. It was a happy day for Kiyo, but a bittersweet one for Sadako. Kiyo said to Sadako, as she was preparing to leave the hospital, "I feel very bad for you, Sadako. We worked so hard to complete a thousand cranes so that our wish would come true. You finished folding one thousand cranes!"

"*O-ne-e-chan*, I'll fold another thousand cranes," replied a saddened Sadako.

Now she was alone. As she stared at the empty bed next to hers, she often cried from loneliness and fear.

But Sadako never lost her thoughtfulness and kindness to others. One day when Masahiro visited her, she took him to the hospital cafeteria and bought him *udon* (noodle soup). On another occasion, Sadako bought ice cream for her younger brother, Eiji, and her sister, Mitsue.

By mid-September, Sadako was too weak to go home for her usual weekend visit. This disappointed her terribly, especially since she had already folded a thousand paper cranes. "I need to fold another thousand cranes," Sadako said to herself. Convinced and determined that this was the answer to her problem, she renewed her ambition to complete a second thousand. At this time, because of the lack of paper, she folded them in smaller size, using a needle. And because she had very little stamina, the cranes took longer to fold. But no matter how long or how difficult, Sadako was determined to succeed in folding another one thousand cranes.

Sadako's parents were keenly aware of why she was folding the cranes, but when they learned that she was going to fold another thousand, they worried that such an arduous task would worsen her condition. Mrs. Sasaki was especially troubled because she noticed that the purple areas now covered almost every part of Sadako's body, and when she went to brush her daughter's hair, handfuls of it would come out with each stroke of the brush.

Sadako's symptoms were exactly like those of her many friends who were contaminated with the Atomic Bomb Disease and eventually died a painful death, so the reality of Sadako's condition was undeniable. "Is this to be my Sadako's fate?" Mrs. Sasaki could not help thinking.

Sadako, on one of her
weekend outings.

eight

CAN'T FOLD ANY MORE

By early October, Sadako was in such a poor condition that she could no longer continue to fold her paper cranes. She had folded about 1,500 cranes, which now filled her room. Time and time again she tried to fold more, but it required too much effort.

There were periods when she found it difficult even to breathe or walk. Each day, she suffered numerous symptoms related to her disease, including high fevers, swelling of the glands, aching muscles and bleeding gums. Much of each day she had to remain in bed.

At the end of each working day Mrs. Sasaki would go directly to the hospital. Normally, she would stay at Sadako's bedside overnight, but there were days when she was obligated to go home to attend to her other three children. One such evening she told Sadako that she had to go home to take care of the family. This made Sadako very upset, but she tried to hide her real feelings by replying, "It's all right, Mama, I understand." When Mrs. Sasaki saw her daughter's eyes sad with tears, she said, "I won't leave you, dear, so long as you're crying. Listen, my darling Sadako, I promise that after today I will stay with you every night, okay?" Mrs. Sasaki did indeed keep her promise, and never once did she miss an evening at the hospital until Sadako's death.

Sadako had become very dependent on her mother's doting attention. Not only did she look forward to her visits, but she enjoyed being treated like a princess; it made her feel secure and loved. She even made a point of not eating her supper until her mother was at her bedside. Though she had become quite dependent on her mother, Sadako always maintained her pleasant and considerate temperament. Once Mrs. Sasaki had a particularly difficult day and complained of a severe headache. "Let me take a little rest on your bed, Sadako," she said, and then proceeded to lie next to her daughter and take a brief nap. Some time later, Sadako gently woke her mother up. Sadako was now standing next to the bed, a headache remedy and glass of water in hand.

Mrs. Sasaki was very touched by her daughter's concern for her, especially since she knew how great an effort it was for her extremely sick daughter to perform this act of kindness. As she took the medicine that Sadako had brought her, she felt a tremendous flush of pride and gratitude. Slowly her eyes began to fill with bittersweet tears.

By mid-October, Sadako was permanently confined to her bed. Now she was in constant pain with extensive swelling in her joints and dangerously high fevers most of the time. Dr. Numata examined her and was about to administer a painkiller, but Sadako refused it, explaining that painkillers are not good for the body. "Is that not so?" she asked.

"It's possible, but this would help you relax," said the doctor. But Sadako told the doctor that she didn't need one.

Kenji, a patient across the hall who was two years younger than Sadako, often cried with pain, and then quite regularly received painkiller treatments. One day, that happened while Mrs. Sasaki was with Sadako. Sadako said to her, "Mom, Ken is taking a painkiller again. Painkillers are not good for the body. I am not taking them!" It seemed that Sadako had overheard some adult patients talking about the side effects of certain painkillers and how they might have adverse effects on the heart. Because of this incident, Sadako was determined to avoid painkillers even though she was suffering constantly from severe pain throughout her body.

nine

SADAKO'S LAST MOMENTS

About eight in the morning on October 25, 1955, a dreary, overcast day, the phone rang at Mr. Sasaki's barber shop. He knew it was bad news by the tone of his wife's voice: "Shigeo, hurry, please hurry. Sadako is dying."

A moment of stunned silence, then: "I'll be right there. I'm on my way." Just before he rushed out of the shop, he remembered to call Mr. Nomura at Nobori-cho Elementary School, and to leave a message at Nobori-cho Junior High School informing Masahiro and Mitsue to go to the hospital immediately.

Mr. Sasaki put little Eiji in the basket on the back of his bicycle, and pedaled as fast as he could to the hospital. What he saw when he dashed into Sadako's room was an extremely pale, sickly girl with eyes closed as if asleep, right next to her mother. Gently, Mr. Sasaki called to her, "Sadako, Daddy is here. Can you hear me?"

Slowly, the frail little girl opened her eyes. In a barely audible voice she said, "Oh Daddy. I'm so glad you're here. You know my legs were hurting so much, but the doctor didn't look at them. He examined my stomach instead. Do you think the doctor has given up on me?"

Reassuringly, the father responded, "Certainly not! In fact, I'll go see him right now and find out what this is all about."

Mr. Sasaki went to locate Dr. Numata, and after a brief conversation they returned together to Sadako's room. The doctor gently and carefully examined Sadako's legs and when he had finished he gave her an injection. As the doctor was about to leave, Masahiro came into the room, quickly followed by Mr. Nomura and Mitsue. Masahiro had come by train and Mitsue had ridden on the back of Mr. Nomura's bicycle. A few minutes after their arrival, a group of former students from Sadako's sixth grade came to visit. Within the hour Sadako's room was filled with friends and relatives.

Mr. Nomura approached the bed to get a better look at Sadako. He wondered silently, "What happened to the star runner of the Bamboo Class who was always so active and healthy? Is this frail, sickly looking girl the same Sadako?"

Mr. Sasaki now asked, "Sadako, is there anything you would like to eat?" With her eyes still closed she softly replied, "No, Daddy. Nothing."

"Please, Sadako, try to eat something. You have to get your strength back."

"All right, Daddy. I would like a little *ochazuke*, please." *Ochazuke* is a simple dish of flavored rice mixed with hot tea. It is a typical Japanese treat.

Mr. Sasaki asked his wife to go to the hospital's kitchen and prepare the dish. When Mrs. Sasaki returned with a bowl of freshly made *ochazuke*, she handed it to her husband. Slowly and gently Mr. Sasaki spoon-fed his daughter. She swallowed three spoonfuls of *ochazuke*, and even ate some pickles. In a soft contented voice, Sadako said, *"Oi-shi-i."* (Oh, that tastes so good.) Then she closed her eyes. Those were the last words Sadako spoke.

Mr. Sasaki called for Dr. Numata. He came quickly. He checked Sadako for vital signs, then turned to Mr. and Mrs. Sasaki and gravely said, "She's passed away." The time was 9:57 A.M.

Sadako's funeral service took place on the following day. It was attended by the entire student body of the former Bamboo Class. Sadako's friends and classmates felt extremely sad during the service, and as they looked at her picture on the front of the altar, some started to cry. They felt awkward as they came to the realization that their dear friend Sadako was now dead. Many of them were also angry; after diligently folding over one thousand paper cranes, Sadako still did not regain her health.

In one of the final rituals of the ceremony, Mrs. Sasaki placed a *kokeshi* in Sadako's casket. This was the *kokeshi* wooden doll that the Bamboo Class had given to Sadako and that Sadako had kept by her bedside while she was in the hospital. Then Mr. Sasaki placed hundreds of Sadako's paper cranes in the casket.

Adorned in the cherry blossom kimono and with the paper cranes, Sadako's body looked like a delicate porcelain doll. Then, Sadako's parents distributed remaining cranes, one by one to Sadako's classmates, hoping that Sadako would be remembered by her friends.

Mr. and Mrs. Sasaki thanked the gathered crowd who came to the funeral service. They told the students that they hoped that Sadako's cranes, made with such passion and dedication, would now take their daughter to heaven, from where she could watch over Hiroshima and even the world.

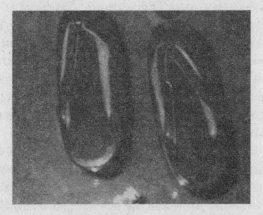

Sadako's kimono slippers

ten

THE CHILDREN'S PEACE STATUE

On October 26, 1955, a small article appeared in the Hiroshima evening newspaper. It briefly reported the death of a young girl who had suffered the effects of atomic bomb radiation. "The death of Sadako Sasaki is the fourteenth death in Nobori-cho Junior High School this year. She had been sick since last fall with the atomic bomb disease. She was exposed to the atomic bomb ten years ago, and now she is gone . . . fourteenth death in this school . . . seventh grader . . . age twelve." The obituary appeared at a time when most of Japan's citizens had come to distance themselves from the horrible memory of war.

Members of the Bamboo Class gathered not long after the funeral to share their grief. Many children felt guilty for not visiting Sadako more often while she was in the hospital, especially after the beginning of their summer vacation. Motivated by their common feelings of remorse, they decided to do something for Sadako.

"What should we do for Sadako?" they asked themselves.

"How about a marker in the Peace Park?" suggested one of the girls. "Yes, to remember Sadako and all other children who died because of *Pika*." They all agreed that a marker sounded like a good idea. "But a marker is expensive," someone else said.

"How on earth can we raise enough money to buy a marker?" The idea of a marker excited them, but the reality of getting the necessary money to buy one frustrated and discouraged them. The means for seventh-graders to raise a large sum of money were obviously very limited. As an alternative, one student suggested bringing flowers to the grave site each month to mark the day Sadako died. All agreed that such a remembrance was not only a good idea, but one that was within their limited financial means. Little did they know that fate was already preparing to alter their plans in a most dramatic way.

Sometime after Sadako's death, the Sasakis hosted a small memorial gathering in their Motomachi home. Mr. Nomura, Sadako's Bamboo Class classmates and a young Mr. Ichiro Kawamoto were invited, along with Sadako's relatives. Mr. Kawamoto was a conscientious man who devoted much of his time as a volunteer, raising support for disabled victims of the atomic bomb. Many of these individuals were unable to work. Mr. Kawamoto frequently spent his own money to help them.

When the bomb fell on Hiroshima, Mr. Kawamoto had been sixteen years old and working at the Hiroshima Bay Power Plant. Fortunately, he was not directly affected by the explosion because the power plant where he worked was some distance away from the center of the city where the bomb fell. Shortly after the bombing, Mr. Kawamoto went into the devastated area as a member of a volunteer rescue team and did everything he could to help the masses of injured men, women and children. His young, impressionable mind never forgot the images of horror he saw on that day, which changed his whole life. Young Mr. Kawamoto vowed that he would dedicate his life to helping the victims of the atomic bomb.

Mr. Kawamoto had related to Mr. Nomura his idea to build a memorial statue for Sadako and all the children who died of the Atomic Bomb Disease. Mr. Nomura then told Mr. Kawamoto of the upcoming memorial gathering at the Sasakis. As a result, Mr. Kawamoto was invited to Sadako's memorial gathering. He was very eager to come to the Sasakis' house and share his idea with everyone. When it came time for Mr. Kawamoto to address the group, he spoke enthusiastically: "Everyone! I believe if we all work together, we can build a memorial statue for Sadako and all the children who died of *Pika*. No one can do it alone. I need your help. We need each other." With great enthusiasm everyone in the gathering agreed.

The rest of the meeting was something of a miracle. Sadako's former classmates, the Bamboo Class, and others inspired by Mr. Kawamoto's idea came together in their common desire to build a memorial statue. A dream had now been born.

"Where and how will we get the money to build a statue?" someone asked. Mr. Kawamoto fixed a serious eye on all those present. "I've got an idea. In a couple of days, the National Principals' Convention will be held at the City Convention Center. They'll be meeting from November tenth to the twelfth. About two thousand principals from all

Mr. Kawamoto

One of the memorial gatherings.

over Japan will attend. Why don't we make up some flyers and distribute them at the convention? We can use the flyers to tell them about Sadako and ask for support in our cause." Sadako's classmates were impressed with Mr. Kawamoto's idea, because they didn't think that they could raise the money to build even a tombstone. Now they were excited by the idea of building a statue in the Peace Park. Mr. Kawamoto's idea was unanimously accepted by the group. Their enthusiasm was rekindled and now they were prepared to put the plan into effect. But the vital question of how to get two thousand flyers printed and distributed in time had to be answered immediately. Mr. Kawamoto said, "First, we need to locate a mimeograph machine." "You can use our school's mimeograph machine," responded Mr. Nomura. Then Mr. Kawamoto looked everybody straight in the eyes and said, "Working as a team we could do it. But there's very little time left before the Principals' Convention, so we must work fast."

Inspired and united by their noble cause, the students immediately put their project into motion. They raised as much cash as they could by pooling their allowance money. Those with artistic ability designed the flyer on the inked, mimeograph plate. Taking turns, they started the time-consuming task of cranking out two thousand flyers, one at a time, by hand. Mr. Nomura and Mr. Kawamoto did their share, too. But on the first day of the convention, they still had not completed the necessary two thousand flyers. It was not until late in the evening on November eleventh that all the flyers were ready for distribution.

This is what the students had written:

LET'S BUILD A STATUE FOR THE CHILDREN OF THE ATOMIC BOMB:

We learned that school principals from all over Japan would be holding their meeting, and therefore we wish to share with you the following story:

Our dear friend, Sadako Sasaki, died on October 25. Since early childhood she was our closest friend. We studied and played together. But in January of this year the innocent Sadako suddenly became sick. After nine long months in the hospital, she died. Knowing that Sadako was aware of her fatal condition has made us very sad. But there is nothing we can do about it now. We do not want her death to have been in vain, so we hope to build a statue for all the children who died of the Atomic Bomb Disease. We are here today to make our project known to you honorable principals, and to ask you to convey our message to all our fellow junior high school students throughout the country, and encourage them to support us. We came today to make this plea.

Hiroshima Municipal Nobori-cho
Junior High School Seventh Graders
All the Classmates of the late Sadako Sasaki

The next and the final day of the convention, four boys and four girls from the group were sent to the convention center to distribute the two thousand flyers. It was a Saturday and the normal school day didn't recess until noon. Foregoing lunch, the eight-member team arrived at the convention center at about 1:15 P.M. They were told by the reception desk that, since the one o'clock session had already begun, they would have to wait until three o'clock, when it would be over.

There was nothing the students could do but wait patiently until the session ended at three o'clock. For this anxious group of young students it was the longest wait of their lives. As three o'clock approached, Mr. Kawamoto arrived to see how things were going and if he could be of any help. He took some time off to help these students. Suddenly the doors to the meeting room swung open and the principals slowly emerged. The eight boys and girls converged on the principals with their flyers. "Please read this. Please. It's important!" Many of the principals were puzzled by this unexpected solicitation. Some ignored the flyers, others put them in their pockets. But quite a few took the time to read them.

One of the principals saw the enlarged picture of Sadako that was held up by one of the students. It was obvious that he was deeply moved by the picture. Handing a contribution to a student, he wished them all good luck with their fundraising.

As the last group of principals left the convention center, the young Sadako devotees knew their campaign had been a success. They had a long way to go, but they were on their way and nothing would stop them!

eleven

THE CIRCLE OF UNITY WIDENS

In December, in the northern cities of Hokkaido and Tohoku, growing numbers of students who had heard about Sadako's story began to show great interest in the memorial statue project. Many of the principals who had read the flyers informed their students about Sadako's tragedy and passed the flyers around, so their students would get involved.

Coincidentally, the year Sadako died was also the year the Atomic Bomb Museum in Hiroshima Peace Memorial Park opened to the public. As visitors to the museum, many of the school principals were vividly reminded of the devastation caused by the atomic bomb. They responded immediately and emotionally to the pain and suffering the bomb had caused when they saw displays depicting such horrors as the black rain that covered Hiroshima after the bombing: men, women and children

Poster used for the fundraising

who had lost their hair to radiation from the bomb, iron beams twisted from the blast; young soldiers with bleeding gums and bodies darkened with purple patches; and the charred remains of homes no longer standing.

The new museum and Sadako's story left a profound impact on the school principals. To motivate their students, they made strong appeals to them to get involved in building the memorial statue. They promoted the virtues of peace, and above all, they used their voices to ask the world never again to use the atomic bomb. Students were so moved when they heard the story of Sadako and the

Hiroshima bombing, they immediately decided unanimously to support the fundraising effort to build a statue. As a result, donations started to pour in from many district junior high schools.

By the end of December, the Student Council of Hokkaido Ashibetsu Junior High School had contributed 400 dollars. Sadako's classmates were overjoyed and their enthusiasm rose to new heights. They were especially pleased when the Ashibetsu students pledged to contact and encourage other junior high school students in Hokkaido to support the memorial project.

By December 31, contributions totaled over 1,200 dollars and kept coming well into the new year!

Encouraged by the outpouring of donations, Sadako's former classmates became more committed and directly involved in the fundraising activities. They formed an official group called *Kokeshi-no-kai* or The Wooden Doll's Association. They gave the association this name in remembrance of the *kokeshi* doll which Sadako had kept at her bedside while in the hospital. The *Kokeshi-no-kai* would include members in addition to the Bamboo Class. In a fundraising effort, members of the *Kokeshi-no-kai* went into the city of Hiroshima and directly solicited contributions.

The circle was widening with each passing day as the *Kokeshi-no-kai* rapidly became a highly recog-

Sadako's brother, Masahiro

Fundraising event

Kiyo Ohkura

nized group in Hiroshima. It attracted support from elementary schools, junior and senior high schools, as well as many other sources. Because of its rapid growth and success, the representatives of elementary, junior and senior high school student councils formed a new group called the Hiroshima Children and Students' Council for the Creation of Peace. Sadako's brother, Masahiro, then a ninth grader at Nobori-cho Junior High School, and Kiyo Ohkura, Sadako's former hospital roommate, also became members of this council.

On March 1, 1956, the council wrote a letter to all the elementary, junior and senior high schools in the nation.

After a very long and painful hospitalization, Sadako died. Yoshito, a fourth grader, also died of the Atomic Bomb Disease. Sadako was only two years old when the atomic bomb was dropped. Immediately after the bomb exploded, her mother put Sadako on her back and, in fear for their lives, ran to Kusunoki-cho. Fortunately, they both survived. However, about a year ago Sadako was diagnosed with the Atomic Bomb Disease. The official medical term for her condition was "malignant acute marrow leukemia." For nine long and painful months, Sadako struggled with this disease and, finally, she died. Every day of her confinement was an unbearable ordeal, but tough, hopeful Sadako tolerated it without complaint. As friends and classmates of Sadako, we frequently visited her at the Red Cross Hospital, where she was always in her bed diligently folding paper cranes. When we asked her why she was folding so many cranes, she replied, "What do you think? I want to get better fast." We will never forget the expression on her face. It was one of absolute determination to get better. Our dear, athletic Sadako was determined to get better, so she could start winning races again. While in the hospital Sadako managed to fold more than 1,000 paper cranes. After she died we each received a folded crane as a memento. We took all the remaining cranes and placed them on her face and chest as she lay in the casket. Then we said our final goodbyes.

*Even to this very day, there are still many res-
idents of Hiroshima dying one after another as a
result of the Atomic Bomb Disease. There are also
children like Sadako and Yoshito who survived
the atomic bomb without a scratch, attended
school like others, only to die eventually because
of that hideous bomb. It was not their war, but
they were forced to pay the price. Why did this happen to us? The people of Hiroshima were not the
only ones injured by the war. Children and students all over the country still suffer from it, and
many of them continue to live in pitiful conditions. Our 10,000 older brothers and sisters who
were burned to death by the atomic bomb didn't
want to die. How horrible must have been their
suffering.*

*Sadako is dead, but to this day she still
doesn't have a traditional altar. And her family
is forced to live in a cold, drafty shack. Dear
Friends! It is our desire to honor the spirit of these
children, many of whom were our dearest friends.
We are saving our allowances and praying that
our dream to build a Statue for the Children of
the Atomic Bomb will become a reality. To this end,
we have banded together in a common cause to
secure the financial means to enable us to achieve
our goal. You undoubtedly know that a project of
such magnitude will be very costly, and this is the
problem we must now resolve.*

Will you please join us? We desperately need your encouragement and support. We ask you from the bottom of our hearts.

The Hiroshima Children and Students' Council
for the Creation of Peace
Masashi Nakamura, Chairperson
Senior at Moto-machi High School
in the City of Hiroshima

This letter succeeded in uniting the city of Hiroshima with schools from all across the nation. As a result, contributions greatly increased. By the end of August, contributions totaled 360,000 dollars; by December when the fundraising campaign officially ended, the council had raised an astounding 450,000 dollars.

In the beginning their noble cause seemed like an impossible dream. Now, after so much hard work, dedication and planning, their dream was within reach. They would build a memorial statue. With the final results greatly exceeding all their expectations, the original group who had come together to honor Sadako could not contain their happiness.

twelve

PRAYER FOR PEACE

With the combined support of more than three thousand schools, plus thousands of individual contributions, the dream to build the memorial statue finally became a reality. The memorial statue would be called *Genbaku-no-Ko-no-Zoh,* or the Statue for the Children of the Atomic Bomb, and Sadako Sasaki would be its model.

On May 5, 1958, Children's Day in Japan, the unveiling ceremony of the memorial took place in the Peace Memorial Park in Hiroshima. All of Sadako's former classmates and others who were actively involved in this project were seated around the base of the statue. Nearby were ten thousand excited children and students representing forty-seven schools.

The Sasaki family was seated along with the members of the original *Kokeshi-no-kai,* the primary driving force for the memorial project.

Children's Peace Statue

The ceremony officially began when Sadako's younger sister Mitsue and younger brother Eiji approached the base of the statue to pull the cord that unveiled the memorial. When the cloth that covered the tall memorial fell to the ground, *Genbaku-no-Ko-no-Zoh* was officially unveiled. Now, the dream of so many had become a reality. Sadako would be remembered forever. On the very top of the statue was the figure of a girl holding a large crane as she looked skyward.

As Mr. and Mrs. Sasaki looked at the sculptured likeness of Sadako atop the memorial statue, they had to restrain themselves from calling out Sadako's name. Silently, they recalled the days when their daughter was a happy, healthy girl.

"Though our Sadako is no longer with us, her spirit lives on, a symbol of peace for all the children of the world!"

Engraved in the dark granite at the foot of the statue are the following words:

> *This is our cry*
> *This is our prayer:*
> *To create peace in the world*

These are the words, the prayers and the cries of the victims of the atomic bomb—past and present. They must be heard and remembered by all the people of the world!

Base of the
statue

To this day, the statue is continually decorated with thousands of paper cranes brought and sent by people throughout the world as symbols of peace. It is an impressive reminder to its visitors that its message is world peace.

Peace must prevail.

About the Author

TAKAYUKI ISHII was born in Tokyo. He converted to Christianity at the age of sixteen. After graduating from Meiji Gakuin University, he was called to be ordained as a Christian minister. He received a Master of Divinity degree from McCormick Theological Seminary in Chicago.

Mr. Ishii has pastored a Japanese-American Church, an African-American church, and several predominantly white congregations in rural and suburban areas. He is presently the pastor of Metropolitan–Duane United Methodist Church, a multicultural congregation in New York City.

Mr. Ishii is married to Jeannette Lynne Bassinger-Ishii, also a United Methodist minister. They have a son, Scott Kenji Ishii.

References

Orizuru no Kodomotachi by Masamoto Nasu

Orizuru no Shojo by Masao Taira

Tobe Senbazuru by Yusuke Tejima

Senbazuru no Negai by Tamiko Yamashita

Kokeshi by Kokeshi no Kai

How to Fold a
Paper Crane

by Camy Condon

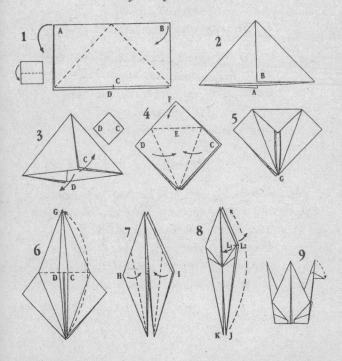

1. Fold a square piece of paper in half horizontally. Then fold A back to bottom center (D), and B forward to front bottom center (C).

2. Your paper should look like this.

3. Pull C (the front) and D (the back) apart all the way until you have a flat diamond (as in small diagram).

4. Fold top layers of C and D inward to center line at E and fold down F along dotted line.

5. Your paper should look like this.

6. Here's the tricky part: Unfold step 4. Take top layer only at G and pull it up making use of the crease (dotted line). This allows points C and D to fold back to center line along creases. Turn paper over and repeat steps 4, 5 and 6, ignoring new flap topped by point G.

7. With split at bottom, fold H and I inward so that edges meet center line. Turn paper over and repeat.

8. Temporarily open flaps at L₁ and L₂. Pull J up to top between flaps and close flaps (L₁ and L₂). Repeat with K. Fold down head. Fold down wings.

The Song

GENBAKU-O-YURUSUMAJI

The first verse in Japanese:

Furusato–no–Machi Yakare
Miyori–no–Hone Umeshi
Yake Tsuchi–ni Ima–wa Shiroi Hana–Saku
Ah, Yurusumaji
Gen–Baku–o Warera–no–Machi–ni.

In translation:

My sweet home, my sweet home has been burned down;
I have buried my loved ones in the once uncharred ground.
Now, many white flowers are blooming;
O we must prevent use of Atomic Bombs;
O never again allow that Atomic Bomb,
In our sweet, sweet, homeland!

原爆を許すまじ

浅田石二 作詞
木下航二 作曲

『ヒロシマの旅』（広島県歴史教育者協議会・「ヒロシマの碑」建設委員会・
広島県高校生平和ゼミナール編，平和文化，1983年発行）より転載
JASRAC 出9709024-701

97